Kindle Paperwhite

Owner's Manual

From Basic Information to Professional Knowledge

Disclaimer

While the author has taken utmost efforts to ensure accuracy of the written content, all readers are advised to follow information mentioned herein at their own risk. The author cannot be held responsible for any personal or commercial damage caused by misinterpretation of information. All readers are encouraged to seek professional advice when needed.

A Quick Glance into This EBook

You may have recently bought a brand new Kindle Paperwhite device, but you do not have much idea about operating it. Or you may have owned the Kindle device for quite some time, but cannot do more on it than just the basics. Whatever the case may be, this eBook will let you explore your Kindle Paperwhite from the surface right down to the depths of it. When you have finished reading this book, you will become an expert with your Kindle Paperwhite, will be able to operate it effectively and will utilize it to the utmost.

As of now, you are just one step away from learning the secrets of the Kindle Paperwhite. Just turn the page and discover what your incredible Kindle Paperwhite has in store for you.

Contents

Getting to know your Kindle Paperwhite

Switch On Kindle Paperwhite

When you receive your device for the first time, it is time to take it out of the box and switch it on. To start using your Kindle Paperwhite, press and hold the **Power** button that is found on the bottom of your tablet.

After you switch on your tablet, you will be guided to a screen that'll ask you to confirm your preferred language.

If you want to switch off your Kindle Paperwhite completely when boarding an airplane or you don't want to use your tablet for a long time, press and hold the Power button for a few seconds until your Home Screen goes blank. You can then release the hold and your device will be switched off completely.

Your Kindle Paperwhite will automatically go to sleep if you don't use it for a long time. You can see a screensaver displayed on your screen when your device is in sleep mode. If you want to put your device to sleep, press and release the power button quickly. You can wake up your tablet by pressing the Power button again.

Just in case your tablet does not switch on or becomes unresponsive while you are using it, you can easily restart it by pressing and holding the Power button for at least 20 seconds.

Touchscreen Features

Your new Kindle Paperwhite offers a number of amazing touchscreen features that help you perform lots of actions with just a simple tap or swipe of your finger. If you want to open an item on your Home Screen, simply tap the icon to perform the action.

Onscreen keyboard

Your device also has an onscreen keyboard that appears when you have to "type in" text such as when you tap the Search button. The onscreen keyboard appears at the bottom of your screen and you can use the appropriate keys to enter your selection.

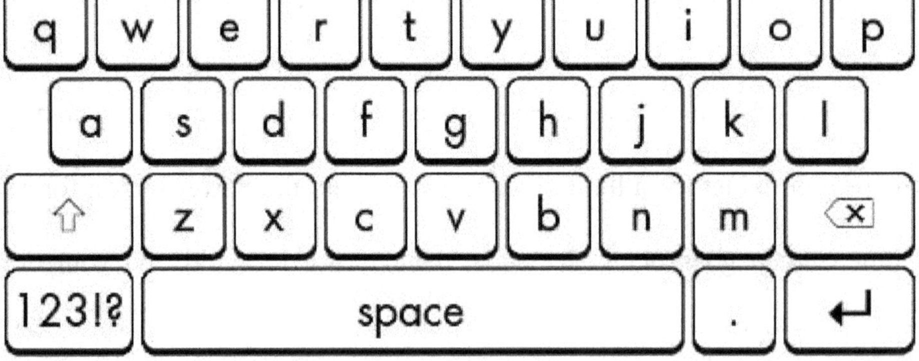

Kindle Paperwhite also allows you to enter diacritics and other special characters using the onscreen keyboard. If you need to display these characters, all you have to do is press and hold the intended letter's key. For example, you can press and hold the letter "n" to display, ñ, or ň on your screen. You can do it for any letter as shown in the figure below.

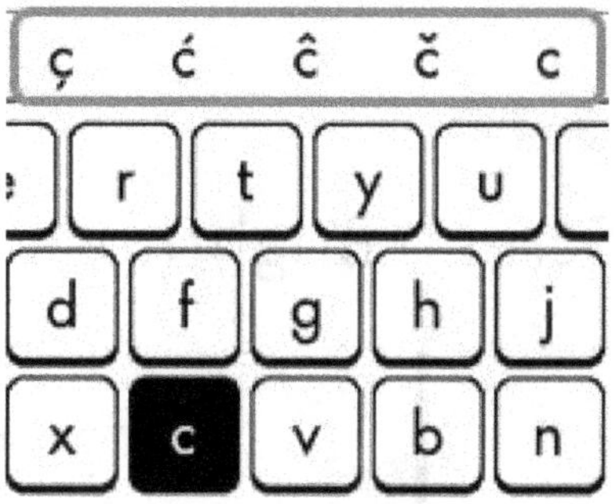

Accessing the Toolbar

You can tap the top of your screen to reveal a tool bar and it will look something like this.

Note, settings and options you see in the toolbar also depend on what you are viewing at that point in time.

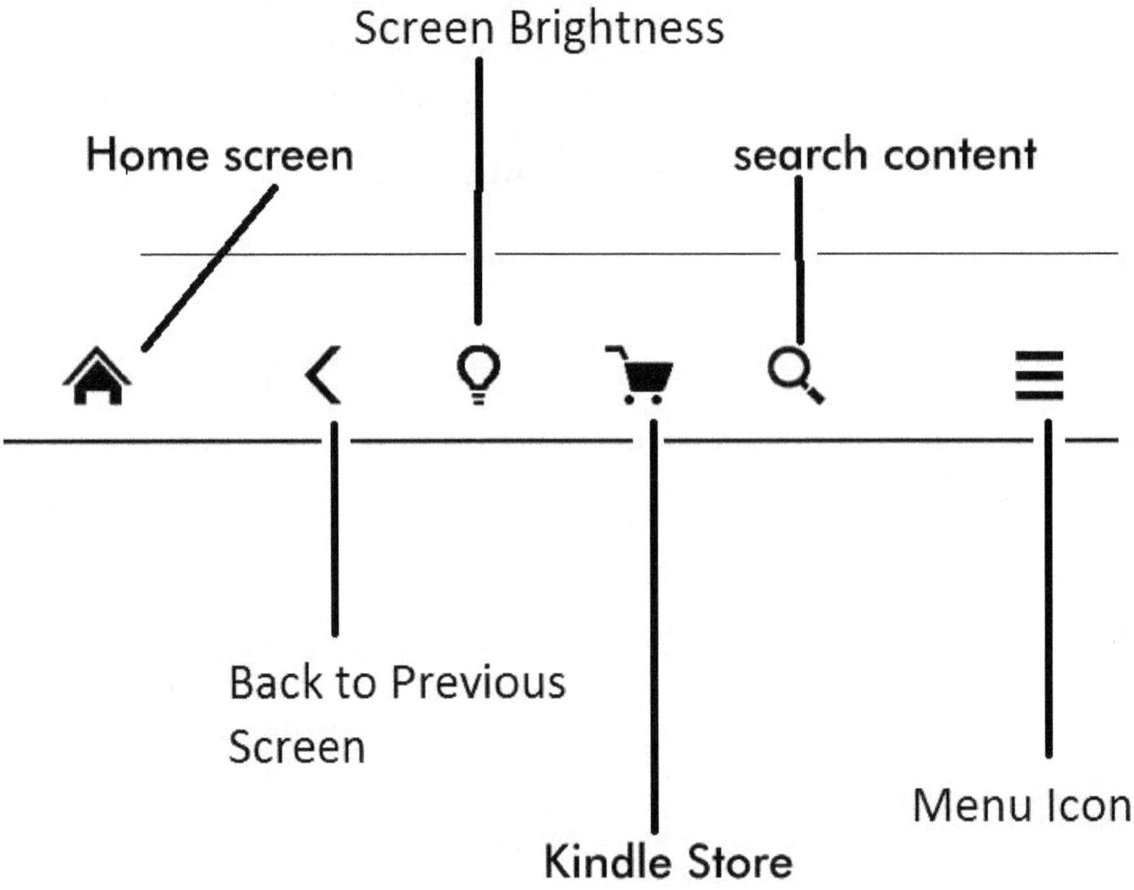

The Back button is a useful tool to track your previous steps.

Screen brightness can easily be adjusted by sliding your finger along the scale. Tap + to increase brightness and tap – to lower screen brightness.

Your tablet needs to connect to a 3G or Wi-Fi network to go to the Kindle Store.

The Search button helps you find things on your device and in the Cloud. Once you enter your search term, tap the Arrow button to the right side of the Search bar to see the results. You can tap the tiny X on the right side of your search bar to exit the search menu.

The Menu button displays a list of options depending on what you're currently doing on your tablet.

The Basic Set Up Process

Selecting Your Preferred Language

You can choose your language using the dialog box that appears on the screen.

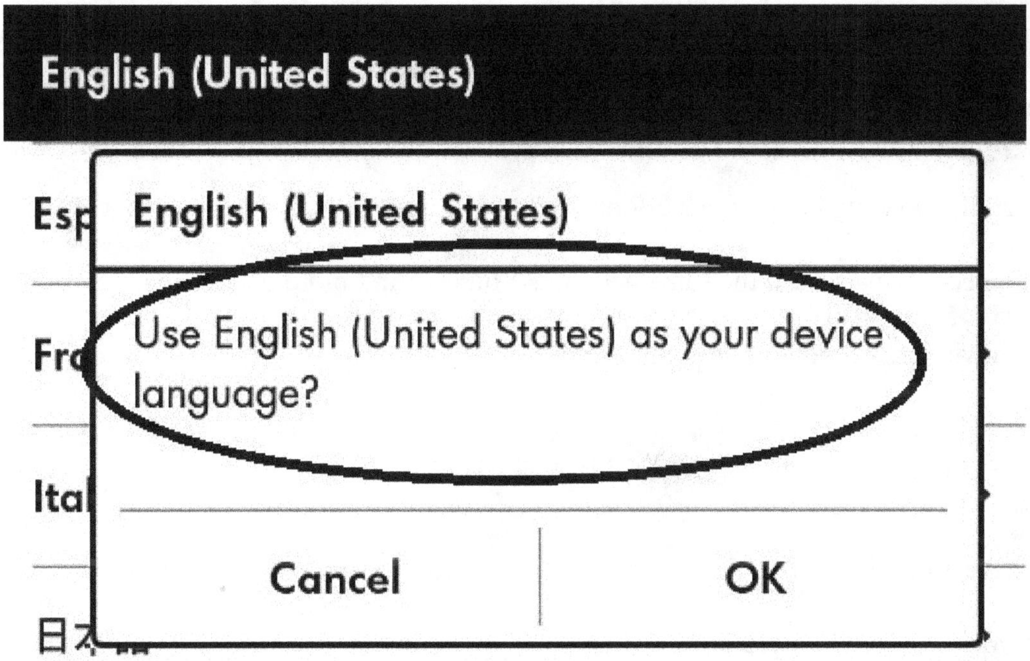

Setting up your preferred language can take a few moments to set up. Once this is complete, tap **Get Started** on the menu that appears on your screen.

Connecting to a Wi-Fi Network

Your Kindle Paperwhite will then ask you to connect to a Wi-Fi network. Remember, connecting your device to a Wi-Fi network can help you do a lot more with your eBook reader. You can download exciting content on your tablet using a wireless network. Your Kindle Paperwhite also comes in a 3G model that can connect to the internet even if you are not close to a Wi-Fi hotspot.

To connect to a wireless network Tap **"Connect to Wi-Fi"** from the message that appears on your Kindle Paperwhite screen. You will then find a list of available networks on your screen and tap the name of the Wi-Fi network that you want to join. You need to enter a password if you want to connect to a secure network.

Use the onscreen keyboard to enter the Wi-Fi network password. Tap **123!?** if you want to enter numbers or symbols. You can tap **ABC** to return to the normal keyboard. Just in case you cannot connect to a secure network, contact the person who is responsible to manage your network.

What's really amazing is that your eBook reader will automatically connect to a Wi-Fi network when it detects signals from the same network. You can find more details about connecting your tablet to a wireless network later in this eBook.

How You Can Register Your Device

You'll have to register your Kindle Paperwhite before you can start shopping for content. To register your device, you need to first connect to your Amazon.com account. Go to Amazon.com and then select **"Use an existing Amazon account"** or **"Create a new account"** depending on whatever applies to your situation. Follow the instructions that appear on the screen to complete the registration process.

If you need to create a new Amazon account to register your device, you'll also have to enter the payment method you'll use when you are shopping for digital content from your device. Just in case your device is already registered, you'll only have to confirm your account. This can happen if you've just purchased your Kindle Paperwhite from Amazon.com.

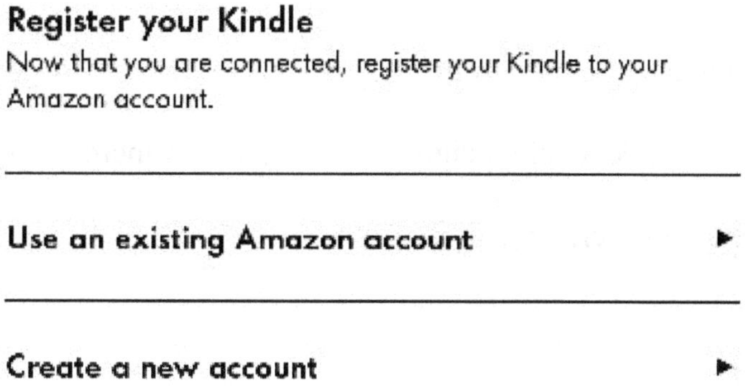

Register your Kindle
Now that you are connected, register your Kindle to your Amazon account.
Use an existing Amazon account
Create a new account

Get Familiar with Status indicators

The status bar displayed at the top of your Home screen gives you a good idea about the status of your Kindle Paperwhite. You can tap the top of your screen to reveal the toolbar.

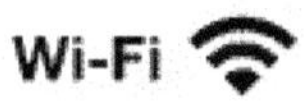

Wireless status indicators

You can download content to your Kindle Paperwhite whenever and wherever you want if you are connected to a wireless network as shown by the figure above. Your Kindle can connect to internet via the built-in Wi-Fi capability or 3G connectivity. Remember, the more bars you have on your wireless status indicator, the better download speed you can achieve.

The 3G icon 3G appears next to the bars only if you have Kindle Paperwhite 3G.

If you see an airplane icon in the status bar, your device is in Airplane Mode and you cannot connect to a wireless network.

Battery status indicator

The Kindle battery indicator shows your battery charge. Don't forget to turn off wireless connectivity if you have weak wireless signals because it can increase power consumption and deplete your battery charge faster.

Activity indicator

You can see an activity indicator in the top left corner of your screen when your device is scanning or connecting to a wireless network. This icon also appears when you are downloading content to your device.

The activity indicator also appears while your device is syncing or checking for new items. You can also find it when you are trying to search for an item or want to open a large PDF file.

Parental Controls indicator

You can see a parental control indicator when Parental Controls are enabled for your Kindle Paperwhite. Setting up Parental Controls gives you a chance to restrict the use of your tablet. You can use parental controls to prevent kids from browsing the web or searching for content from the Kindle Store.

A Look at the Main Features

If you're reading this chapter, you've probably completed the basic Kindle Paperwhite setup process which includes choosing your preferred device language, connecting to a Wi-Fi network, as well as registering your tablet to a valid Amazon account.

If you haven't done any of these steps yet, you can do so by going back to the Home screen right now. Once you reach the Home Screen, tap **Set Up Your Kindle**, and follow the instructions that appear on the screen. Remember, once you complete the basic setup process, the **"Set Up Your Kindle"** message will no longer appear on your device's Home screen.

Your shiny new Kindle Paperwhite is one of the most fascinating devices in the Kindle Line of products; maybe even the best for quite a lot of people. It has really amazing features and lives up to the expectations that Amazon fans have from their products.

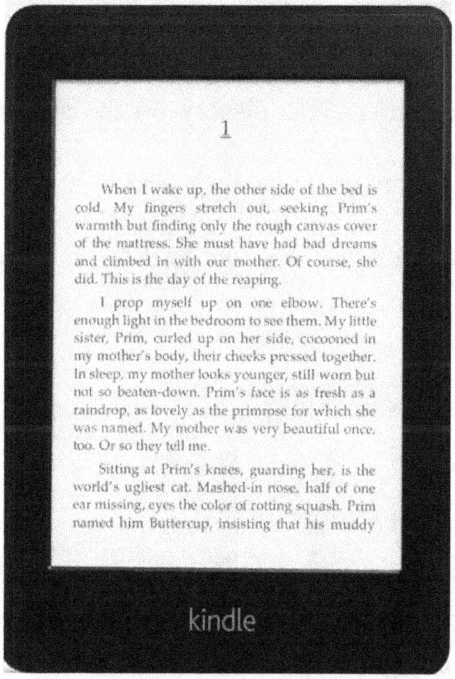

Figure 1: Kindle Paperwhite

Here is a look at some of the facts that have surged the popularity of the Kindle Paperwhite.

1. High resolution screen
2. Increased contrast for sharper text
3. Absolutely free 3G connectivity
4. A built-in light which illuminates the screen really well whether you read in bright sunlight or under the blanket.
5. Stunning battery life which lasts as long as 8 weeks
6. Downloadable books from a really huge collection

The Display

The Display of Amazon Paperwhite is the most notable feature of the device. Compared to previous Amazon's eReaders, the resolution has been increased by a massive 60%. So what you get out of this is a really sharp and clear display on the screen. The contrast has also been increased by 25% so that you can read the dark text with ease. The figure below shows a comparison between screens of the Paperwhite and previous generation.

Your Paperwhite will also let you adjust the screen brightness so that your eyes are not affected by the glare or dimness of the screen. The built-in light does not project out the display into your eyes, but just lights it from above so that your eyes do not tire out. This makes the Kindle Paperwhite perfect for reading in all lightning conditions.

Battery Life

The battery life of your Kindle Paperwhite can last a stunning length of time. Yes, it is really surprising, but you should actually try this out for yourself so that you believe it. If you set your light setting at 10, read an hour a day, and turn Wi-Fi off, your Paperwhite will accompany for a full 30 days without you needing to charge it even once. You can even leave the light on all the time, and it will still have no impact on your battery life.

You can fully charge your tablet in less than four hours using the USB cable that comes with your device. Remember, it can take slightly longer than 4 hours to charge your tablet fully in case your battery is completely drained. To charge your tablet, make sure you connect it to a computer using the same USB cable that comes with your device.

How Do You Know if Your Kindle Paperwhite is Charging or Not?

You can see a tiny lightning bolt at the top of your Home Screen when you connect your tablet to a computer. The lightning bolt remains amber while your battery is charging and turns green once it is fully charged.

If you don't want to charge your tablet using a computer, you can buy a compatible Kindle Paperwhite AC adaptor to charge your device. Your Kindle Paperwhite can be charged in less than four hours using this power adaptor.

Viewing Your Home Screen

Your Home Screen is what allows you to view items in your Kindle Library or access items that are stored on your Kindle Paperwhite. You can use your Home Screen to access your device settings and connect to a Wi-Fi network.

There are two ways you can get back to your Kindle Paperwhite Home Screen.

1. Tap the Home icon from any of your settings.
2. Tap the top of your screen to access the toolbar and then tap the Home icon.

Connect to Wi-Fi

1. To connect to a Wi-Fi network, tap the menu icon and then tap Settings.
2. Tap **Wi-Fi Networks** and then tap the network you want to connect to. Make sure you enter the correct password if you want to connect to a secure network.
3. Once you are successfully connected to a Wi-Fi network, you can check the wireless status and signal strength from the top-right corner of your Kindle Paperwhite screen.

Kindle Paperwhite Wi-Fi and 3G

Presently, your Kindle Paperwhite is available in two different models namely Wi-Fi and Wi-Fi + 3G. The 3G model allows you to connect to the internet using a mobile network. Moreover, your Kindle Paperwhite 3G automatically switches to Wi-Fi if it finds a Wi-Fi network with better signals. You will be reconnected to 3G automatically if the Wi-Fi network is no longer reachable.

Remember, you need to connect to a wireless or 3G network if you want to search and shop for content from the Kindle Store.

How Can You Check Whether You Have Kindle Paperwhite Wi-Fi or 3G?

If you want to check what type of device you have, first tap the Menu icon and then go to Settings.

Select the Menu icon again and then tap Device info. You will then see your device type and your wireless/mobile network options will appear under Network Capability.

Kindle Paperwhite and Wireless Networks

You can connect to the internet using the Wi-Fi network at your home or a Wi-Fi hotspot at a public place such as a hotel or your favorite snack bar. Your eBook reader automatically detects wireless networks that are within your range and you can see their names displayed under Wireless networks.

Your device must be within the range of the particular Wi-Fi network you want to connect to. Remember, even if you are using Kindle Paperwhite 3G, you can achieve faster download speeds when you use a Wi-Fi connection.

Choosing a Wi-Fi Network

If you want to see the Wi-Fi networks that are available, first go to your Home Screen and then tap the Menu icon. Tap settings and then go to **Wi-Fi Networks** to see a list of connections that are available in your region. You have to be patient as this list can take some time to appear.

Remember, networks that appear with a lock icon require a password to connect.

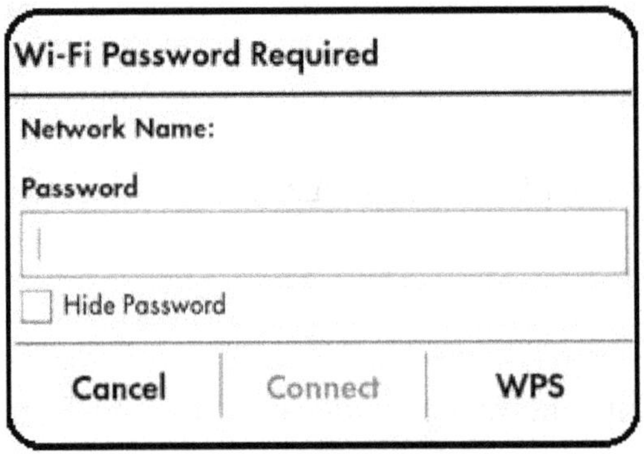

Wi-Fi Standards and Authentication Methods

Your device can connect to wireless networks or hotspots that use 802.11b, 802.11g, or 802 authentication methods. Additionally, Kindle Paperwhite also supports the following networks.

1. EAP-PEAP with MSCHAPv2

2. EAP TTLS with MSCHAP v2
3. EAP-TTLS with PAP

Can I Add a New Wi-Fi Network Manually?

In case your Wi-Fi network does not appear in the list of detected networks, you can still connect to the wireless network manually.

To add a network manually, make sure that you are within range of the network. You also need to know the network name and password.

1. Go to your Home screen and then tap the **Menu icon**.
2. Go to **Settings** and then tap **Wi-Fi Networks** to display a list of Wi-Fi networks that are available in your region.
3. Tap **Other** from the list that appears on the screen and then enter the **Network Name**.
4. Tap **Password** to enter the Wi-Fi password / Network Key if applicable.
5. Tap **Connect** to exit set up.
6. You can choose **Set Up,** then **Advanced** to enter network information manually just in case you see an **Unable to Connect** message.
7. If nothing works, try connecting to a different wireless network or contact the person who manages your network.

Connect to 3G

Kindle Paperwhite 3G models can connect to the internet using 3G connectivity. If you use 3G to browse the internet, you can see one of the three indicators namely 3G, EDGE, or GPRS in the upper right corner of your tablet's screen.

Your Kindle Paperwhite automatically turns 3G off when a Wi-Fi network is available. If you switch off the Wi-Fi network or move out of its range, your Kindle Paperwhite will automatically switch back to 3G.

Airplane Mode

Your Kindle Paperwhite cannot connect to a Wi-Fi or 3G network if Airplane Mode is turned on. You can also see an airplane icon at the top of your screen when Airplane Mode is on. To switch off Airplane Mode, first go to your Home Screen.

Tap **Menu**, and then go to **Settings.** Tap the "On" icon that appears to Airplane Mode to enable wireless connectivity. The Airplane mode will then be turned off.

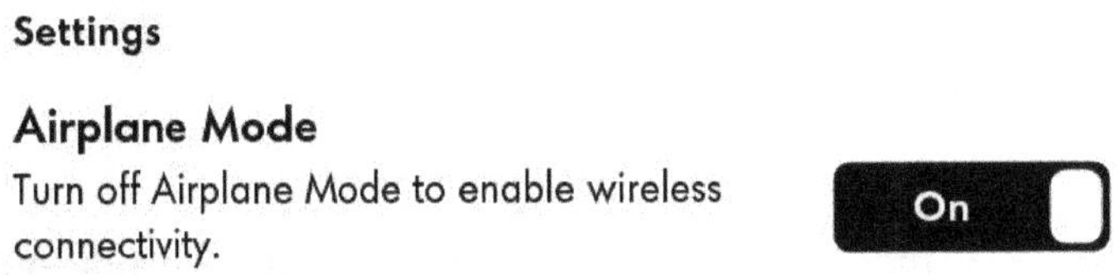

Shopping from the Kindle Store

You can buy digital content from the Kindle Store once you connect to a Wi-Fi network. To go to the Kindle Store, first go to your Home Screen and then tap the Shop icon  .

You can search for your favorite books and magazines and then tap **Buy** to purchase the item. The items you buy are stored in your Kindle Library and you can download the content to your device whenever you want.

For more information on this topic, don't forget to check out the section on **Managing Your Content**.

Reading Books on Kindle Paperwhite

Your tablet does not need to connect to a wireless network to read books that are downloaded on your device. Go to your Home Screen and then tap **Device** to view the entire collection of items available on your device.

If you want to start reading a book, simply tap the icon to open it. Swipe across the screen to turn pages and more details on reading books on Paperwhite is coming up later in this eBook.

How You Can Sync Your Kindle Paperwhite

Once you connect your tablet to a wireless network, you can sync your device to receive content you were reading on other Kindle devices or apps. You can use a number of methods to sync your device.

First go to your Home Screen and then tap the Menu icon. Tap **Sync and Check for Items** and all the new items should start downloading to your device. More updates on Syncing your Kindle Content can be found on the later pages.

How You Can Adjust Screen Brightness

It is very important to maintain optimal screen brightness while reading on your new Kindle Paperwhite. You can use the adjustable screen light from the toolbar to increase or decrease screen brightness. If you want to change screen brightness while reading, tap the bulb icon that appears on your screen.

You can then slide your finger to the left or the right side to adjust screen brightness. Low screen brightness works best for rooms having low lighting. You can go for higher settings if your room has bright lights.

How You Can Remove Content from Your Kindle

Once you have finished reading a book on Kindle Paperwhite, you can remove it from your device. Remember, the content you remove from your device still remains saved in the cloud and you can access it anytime from **Manage Your Kindle**.

To remove a book from your Kindle Paperwhite, first go to your Home Screen and then tap the book cover or title. Select **Remove from Device** from the menu that appears on the screen. If you want to learn how you can permanently remove content from your device and the cloud, don't forget to check out the chapter titled **Manage your Kindle Content**.

Setting Up Parental Controls

You can set up parental controls to not only restrict the use of your device, but you can also use it to limit access to the Kindle store and web browsing. However, you can buy books from the

Kindle store using your computer and deliver it to your Kindle Paperwhite even when parental locks are applied.

To set up parental controls, first go to your Home screen and then tap the menu icon.

Select settings and then go to Device Options.

Tap Parental Controls and select Off to set up a password to restrict access to the Kindle Store, Web Browsing and Amazon Cloud.

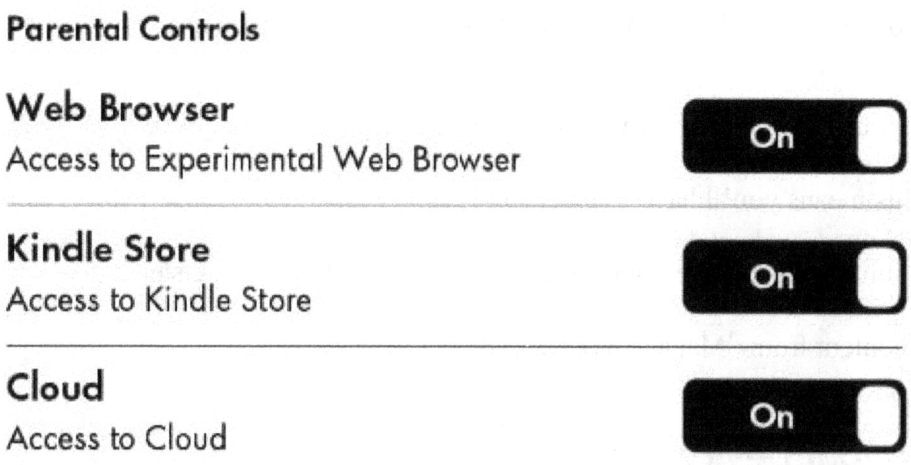

Once you select Off, enter your desired password and tap OK to complete the set up process. You will then see a lock icon at the top of your screen which indicates that parental controls are applied.

Kindle Paperwhite and Device Passcode

You can set a "passcode" to control unauthorized access to your Kindle Paperwhite. Once you set a passcode, you'll have to enter the same code to unlock your device if it goes to sleep or is powered off. Here's a simple way to set up a passcode.

1. First, go to your Home Screen and then select the Menu icon.
2. Tap **Settings** and then select **Device Options**.
3. Tap **Device Passcode** and then enter your desired password.
4. Tap OK once you confirm your password to complete the set up process.

Remember, you'll have to restore your device to original factory settings if you forget your passcode. This means you'll have to enter "111222777" as the passcode, which will restore your tablet to default settings. Once your tablet is reset, you'll have to register it again and download your digital content from "Manage Your Kindle."

Changing your Device Name

You can easily change the name of your device to personalize it and make it look different from your other Kindle devices. If you want to change the name of your tablet, first go to the Home Screen and then select Menu.

Go to **Settings** > **Device Options > Personalize your Kindle**. Enter your desired name and then select **Save** to confirm your selection. Your new device name will now be seen in the upper left corner of your device screen.

Highlighting the Differences between Kindle Paperwhite and Other E-Readers

You can surely say that Amazon has truly revolutionized the concept of eBook readers. Before the introduction of Kindle devices, no one ever imagined a device that can change the traditional reading experience. But Amazon's eBook readers have been a real game changer and are actually quite impressive at the first sight.

When you have the first look at the Kindle Paperwhite hardware, you will surely be all smiles. The moment you handle your Paperwhite for the very first time, you'll see that it is a little thinner than its Amazon counterpart, Kindle Touch. Leaving the technical details aside, Paperwhite is a lot more visually appealing than other eBook readers as it has borrowed quite a lot of design attributes from one of the most popular Amazon eBook readers, "Kindle Fire HD."

If you are talking about Kindle Paperwhite's main attractions, you surely cannot ignore the use of E Ink. This technology gives Paperwhite some real advantages over tablet devices such as Apple's iPad 4. Not only you can read eBooks in direct sunlight, but Kindle Paperwhite's screen is easier on your eyes.

Kindle Paperwhite also scores more points when you talk about screen resolution. Paperwhite manages to give a resolution of 212 ppi to make text look absolutely stunning, clear and crisp. Even Paperwhite's battery performance lives up to the mark. As mentioned earlier, your tablet can hang in for about eight weeks with a single battery charge if you use it moderately.

Delving Deeper into Your E –reader

Making Social Connections

How You Can Connect to Facebook and Twitter

You can connect Kindle Paperwhite to your Facebook and Twitter account(s) when you set up your device for the first time. Once you link your eBook reader to your social accounts, you can share your read on your Facebook wall or Twitter feed. Moreover, you can also unlink your accounts whenever you want.

To link your Kindle Paperwhite to Facebook and Twitter, first go to your Home Screen and then select the **Menu** icon. Tap **Settings** > **Reading Options > Social Networks**. Choose **Link Account** and follow the instructions that appear on the screen to complete the set up process.

amazonkindle
Manage Your Social Networks
Link your Facebook and Twitter accounts to seamlessly share excerpts of books to your wall or feed. Messages you share to Facebook or Twitter will be linked back to https://kindle.amazon.com.
twitter
Link Account
facebook
Link Account

Want to Share Your Read With Friends?

If there's anything interesting in a Kindle book that you want to share with your friends on Facebook or Twitter, all you have to do is tap and drag the text on your screen to highlight a passage. Next, tap the top of your screen to reveal the reading toolbar.

Tap Share and enter the comments you want to post on your wall or Twitter feed. Once you finish entering the text, select Share to send the highlight to your Facebook or Twitter account.

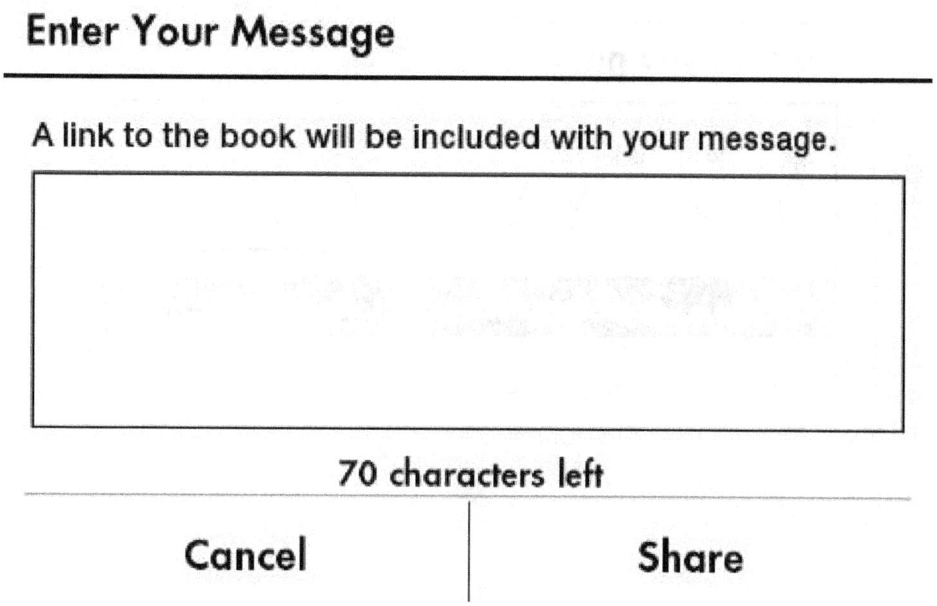

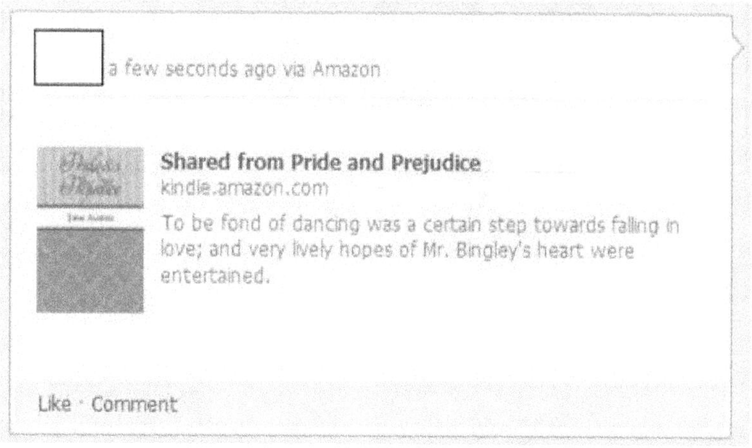

a few seconds ago via Amazon
Shared from Pride and Prejudice
kindle.amazon.com
To be fond of dancing was a certain step towards falling in love; and very lively hopes of Mr. Bingley's heart were entertained.
Like · Comment

Know How You Can Rate, Share and Get Recommendations for Your Books

Once you reach the end of your book, you can tweet or post comments about your read, rate the Kindle book and even get recommendations for a number of additional books. First, tap the top of your screen to reveal the reading tool bar. Tap **Go To** and then select End.

If you want to rate your book, tap the number of stars you want to give. You can also tap Share to let your friends know that you've read the book. There'll also be a page titled **Before you go**, a page where you can find lots of recommendations for your future reads.

Managing Your Content

Your digital content is stored in the Amazon Cloud at **Your Kindle Library as** soon as you make a purchase. You can easily transfer items from the cloud to your Kindle Paperwhite using any one of the following ways.

1. Wireless transfer
2. Transfer using the supplied USB cable
3. Using the Personal Documents Service and Kindle Email ID
4. Transfer with the help of Send-to-Kindle Application for PC, Mac, and web browsers

Wireless Transfer

All items you buy from the Kindle store are automatically stored in the Amazon Cloud and you can access them easily by tapping the Cloud tab displayed on your Home Screen.

If you want to download items through wireless transfer, you'll have to first connect your tablet to a wireless network. Once you are done, tap the Cloud icon on your Home Screen to see the contents in your Kindle Library.

Tap your desired item to start downloading it to your device. You can tap the device tab to view content that is downloaded from the cloud.

Transfer Content from the Kindle Cloud Using the Supplied USB Cable

You can directly transfer Kindle store content from your Macintosh or Windows computer to your Kindle Paperwhite using the supplied USB cable. When you plug your tablet to the computer, it will appear as a removable mass storage device.

If you've already purchased the content from the Kindle Store, first visit **Manage Your Kindle** from your computer browser and locate the desired items in the Kindle Library.

Click **Actions** that appears next to your book title and then select **Download & transfer via USB**.

You will then be prompted to select your Kindle Device. Make sure you select the right Kindle because your digital content will not open on any other device. Select Kindle Paperwhite and then click **Download**.

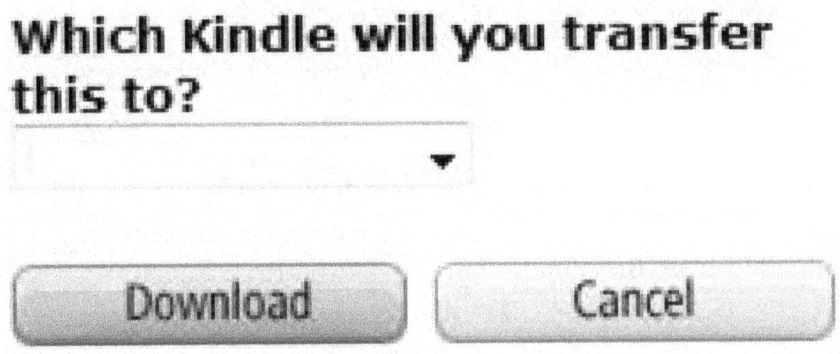

If you haven't purchased the items, go to the Kindle Store using your computer web browser and then select **Transfer via Computer** from the options that appear under **Deliver to.**

Once you select **Transfer Via Computer**, click **Buy now with 1-Click**. You will then be asked to choose your Kindle device in case you have a number of Kindle products linked to the same account. As mentioned earlier, you have to select your Kindle Paperwhite as the content will not open on any other device.

Choose **Save** from the dialog box that appears on the screen to save the file to your Kindle Paperwhite.

Can You Transfer Content Already Stored on Your Computer?

Yes, you can transfer your personal documents on your Mac or Windows computer to Kindle Paperwhite using the supplied USB cable. For this, you have to first connect your tablet to your computer using a USB port.

Kindle Paperwhite will appear in the same location your other external USB devices appear. If you are using a Windows computer, you can find Kindle Paperwhite under **Computer** or **My**

Computer. Similarly, if you are using a Macintosh computer, your device will appear on your desktop.

Once you locate your device on the computer, open the Kindle drive and identify the **Documents** folder inside your Kindle Paperwhite. Locate the desired files on your computer and copy them directly to the Document folder on your Kindle Paperwhite. You can disconnect your device once you finish copying all the files. The content you transfer from your computer appears under the device tab on your Kindle Paperwhite.

Remember, Kindle Paperwhite only supports files:

1. That are transferred to the documents folder
2. That are free of digital rights management (DRM) software
3. That are a supported file type

Supported File Formats	.bmp .doc .epub .gif .html .jpeg .mobi .pdf .png .txt

Transfer Content with your Send-to-Kindle E-mail Address

You will be given a special Send-to-Kindle e-mail address when you register your device. This address can be used to transfer personal documents to your Kindle Paperwhite, however you have to ensure that:

1. You have added the sender email ID to your **Approved Personal Document E-mail List.**
2. The document you transfer is a supported file type.
3. You have entered the correct Send-to-Kindle e-mail address.

To check your **Send-to-Kindle E-mail address**, go to your Home Screen and then tap **Menu**. Go to Settings > **Device Options > Personalize your Kindle**. You can find your email ID under **Send-to-Kindle E-mail address**.

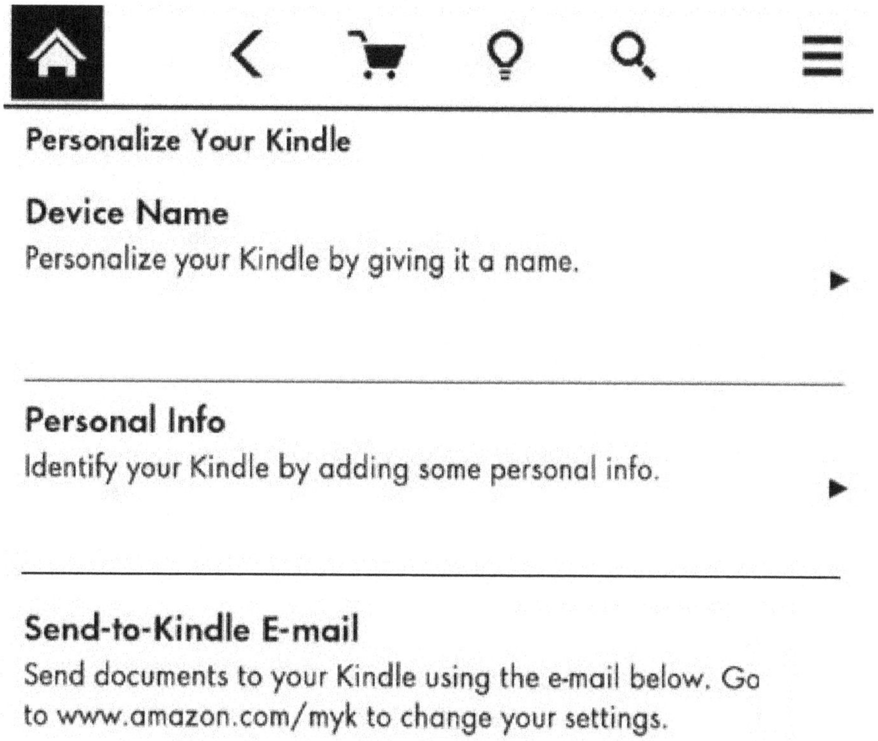

Use "Send to Kindle" Application for PC, Mac or Other Web Browsers

"Send to Kindle" is an interesting app you can install on your computer, Mac or web browser to directly send documents to your Kindle Paperwhite. Once you install this app, you can send documents directly from your computer or your web browser to your tablet. You can also send documents to your Kindle Library and access them by tapping the Cloud tab under Docs on your Kindle Paperwhite.

Sync Your Content Across All Your Kindle Devices & Apps

What's really interesting is the fact that Whispersync is turned on by default on your Kindle Paperwhite and you can use it to sync content across all your kindle devices and apps. To sync your content, first visit https://www.amazon.com/manageyourkindle and then select **Your Kindle Account.**

Select **Manage Your Devices > Device Synchronization** and make sure **Whispersync Device Sychronization** is turned on.

Reading Your Books

Revealing the Reading Toolbar

Kindle Paperwhite gives you a chance to enjoy an incredible reading experience like never before. You can access the reading tool bar by tapping the top of your screen. The reading toolbar has a number of options that help you customize font type, font size, line spacing and page margins while reading a book on Kindle Paperwhite.

Remember, you can only change the fonts and line spacing while reading a book and text size in menus and other screens cannot be changed. Similarly, you cannot alter the appearance of PDF documents while viewing them on Kindle Paperwhite.

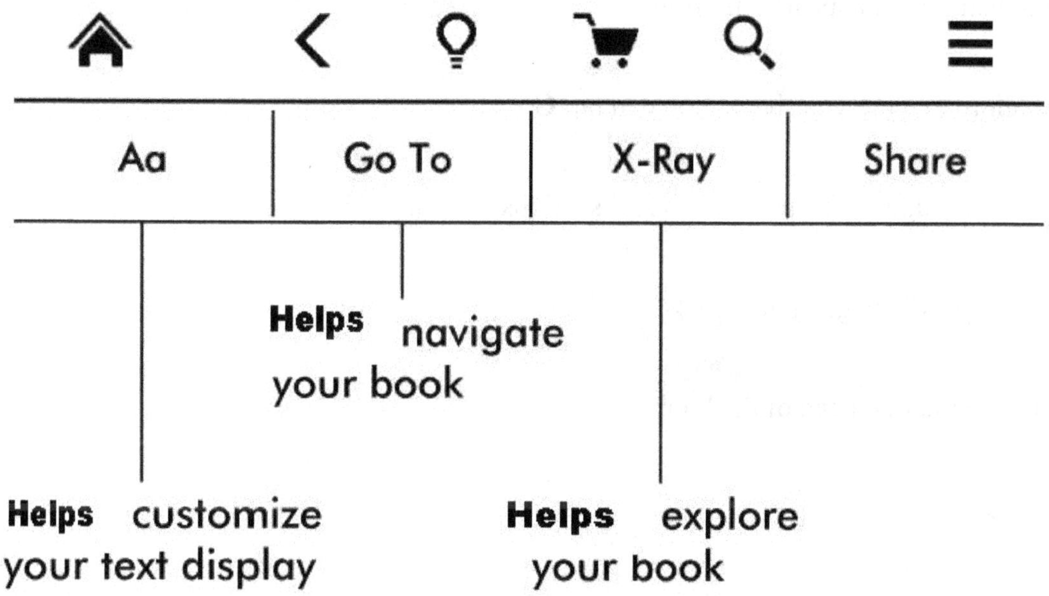

You can select **Aa** from your reading toolbar to customize fonts. When you tap **Aa,** you'll see a menu like this.

Note: Publisher Font appears only if the publisher has specified a font for the book.

If you want to explore your book, you can tap **Go To** and:

1. Browse through different chapters and sections in your book.

2. Go to a specific page number.

3. Return to the first page of the book.

Tap zones

The EasyReach feature in Kindle Paperwhite helps you turn pages even if you are holding the device with just one hand.

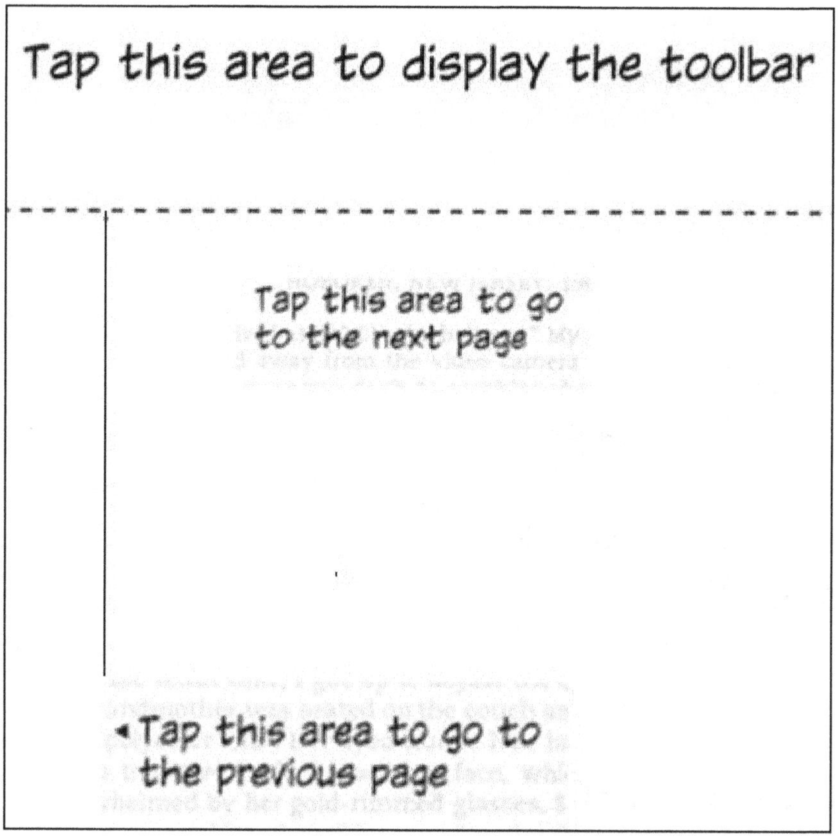

Tapping anywhere in the display area will automatically take you to the next page. You can tap the left side of your screen to go to the previous page. Tap the top of your screen to reveal the reading toolbar.

If you want to change the screen orientation, you can do so easily by tapping the Menu icon and then selecting Portrait or Landscape.

Kindle Paperwhite and X-Ray

As its name suggests, the X-Ray feature in Kindle Paperwhite allows you to explore your book in detail. You can tap X-Ray to reveal the ideas, person or topic discussed in your book. While X-ray is an amazing feature, it is not available for all Kindle books. You can know whether or not your Kindle book has X-ray enabled by looking at its product details.

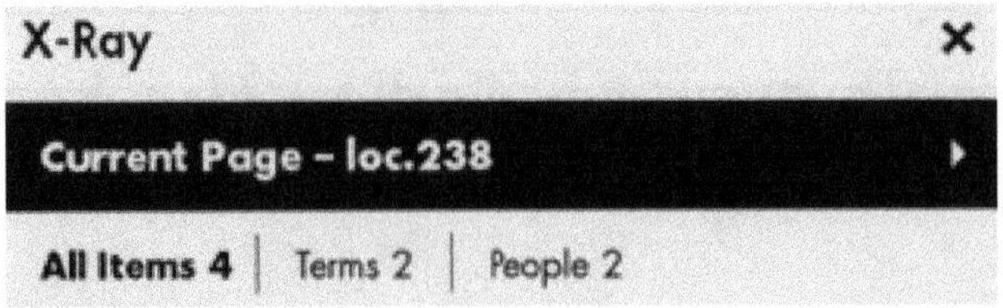

Product details

- **Format:** Kindle Edition
- **File Size:** 2116 KB
- **Print Length:** 57 pages
- **Publisher:** Riley Weber (16 Aug 2012)
- **Sold by:** Amazon Media EU S.à r.l.
- **Language:** English
- **ASIN:** B008YYLYVS
- **Text-to-Speech:** Enabled ▾
- **X-Ray:** Enabled ▾
- **Average Customer Review:** ★★★½☆ ▾ (262 customer reviews)

Want to Add or Remove Bookmarks from Your Kindle Book?

You can place a number of bookmarks in your favorite Kindle Book or PDF document. Here's a simple way to add a bookmark. First go to the desired page in your Kindle book and then tap the right corner of your Kindle Paperwhite screen. A tiny bookmark icon will appear in the corner. If you want to remove your bookmark(s), simply tap the bookmark icon again and your bookmark will be removed.

If you want to view the bookmarks you've added, first tap the top of your screen and then tap the Menu icon. Select **View Notes & Marks** to see the list of bookmarks.

Highlight Your Favorite Passages While Reading a Book

You can highlight your favorite passages and text while reading a Kindle book. If there's anything you want to highlight, simply tap and hold a single word until you see a marker. Drag the markers to the desired spot and then select **Highlight**. You can highlight text in your Kindle content. Your highlighted text will appear with a gray background.

If you are not happy with the text you've highlighted, you can also remove it easily. Just tap and hold the highlighted passage until you see a message on the screen. Select Delete and the highlight will be removed.

Interacting With Words

You can look up word definitions while reading a Kindle book. Simply tap and hold a word to see a small definition. You can select **Show Full Definition** to see the definition in the dictionary. If you want to return to the page you were reading, simply tap the back button in your toolbar. (You can access the basic toolbar by tapping the top of your screen.)

Kindle Paperwhite now supports dictionaries in the following languages.

1. Brazilian Portuguese
2. U.S. English
3. U.K. English
4. French
5. German
6. Italian

7. Japanese

8. Chinese

9. Spanish

View Reading Progress

The **Time To Read** feature on Kindle Paperwhite helps you keep track of your reading speed and you'll know when you can finish reading a particular chapter. To know when you can finish reading a chapter, tap the top of your screen and then select the Menu icon.

Tap **Reading Progress** and then keep track of your progress using Location in Book, Time Left in Book or Time Left in Chapter. Once you set up a reading progress monitor, your progress will be displayed every time you tap the top of your screen while reading.

Get Access to Enhanced Content Features

Kindle Paperwhite also allows you to read Kindle books that contain enhanced **Kindle Format 8** content features. You can access features like Kindle Panel View, zoom in and out of images and even access Kindle Text Pop-Up.

Subscribing to Magazine and Newspapers

You can subscribe and read a newspaper or a magazine on your Kindle Paperwhite through the Amazon's Kindle Store. To start with the subscription process, connect your device to a wireless network and tap the top of your screen. You'll have to tap the Kindle Store icon from the toolbar to go to the store.

Once you go to the Kindle Store, tap **Newspapers or Magazines** to locate and shop for items that are available.

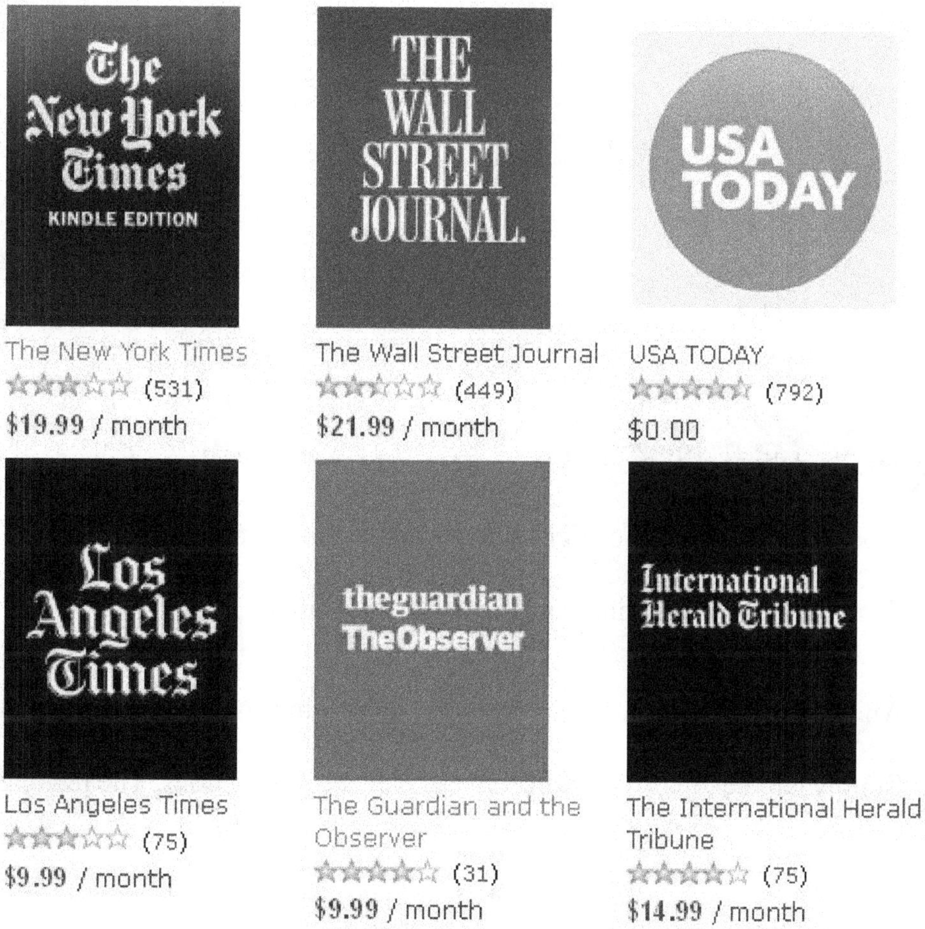

Go to www.amazon.com/manageyourkindle and select your subscription payment method. You can choose Kindle Paperwhite as the device where you want the content to be delivered.

After the content is delivered to your device, you can tap the article or page to start reading. Simply swipe your finger to the left or right side of your screen to turn pages. You can also move from one article to the other by moving your finger up and down.

Kindle Paperwhite also allows you to customize your reading experience while viewing your subscription. Simply tap the top of your screen to display a list of options. The navigation toolbar gives you:

1. The image and preview of the top articles under **Section & Articles.**
2. A chance to change font size, font type and font spacing under **Font options**.

3. A search box to search for your favorite items.

4. You can also save a copy of the entire article to your "My Clippings" that can be accessed from your Home Screen. If you want to save a copy of the article, all you have to do is **Clip This Article**. You can view the articles you have "clipped" by tapping **My Clippings** from your Home Screen.

Access Subscription Content on your Device

You can view the back issues of newspapers and magazines on your Kindle Paperwhite Home screen. Tap **"Periodicals: Back Issues"** to access magazines and newspapers that are stored on your device. However, you have to remember that Kindle Paperwhite deletes content that is more than seven issues old to free valuable storage space on your device.

If you want to retain an issue, press and hold the item under Periodicals**: Back Issues**. Select **Keep This Issue** from the message that appears on the screen.

Troubleshooting Your Device

Your Kindle Paperwhite Screen is not Responding

Restarting your device can help you get rid of problems such as an unresponsive screen. Press and hold the power button for at least 20 seconds. Your screen will go blank but there's nothing to worry about. You can release the button to restart your device. This should help you see your Home Screen again.

You Forget Your Passcode

This can cause a bit of problems as you'll have to restore your tablet to factory settings. **To restore the device to factory defaults**, enter the code **111222777**.

You can also decide to reset your device if you want to delete the entire content from your Kindle Paperwhite. To do this, first go to your Home Screen and then tap the Menu icon. Select Settings > Menu > **Reset Device** to restore default factory settings.

You Cannot Register Your Device

If you cannot register your device, make sure the password you enter is the same password you use to access your Amazon.com account. Remember, passwords are case sensitive and you have to enter the correct letters and symbols while entering your password.

Here's a quick reminder to help you use the onscreen keyboard.

Tap the **123** key to display numbers and special characters on your screen.

Tap the arrow or Shift key to enter uppercase letters

If you've used accented characters in your password, press and hold the basic letter key until you see the special characters on your screen.

Your Screen Becomes Unresponsive Quite Often

If your screen becomes unresponsive even after restarting the device, make sure you charge your device and then restart it again. On the other hand, if your screen becomes too bright or too dark, try adjusting the screen brightness by selecting the Screen Light Icon from your toolbar.

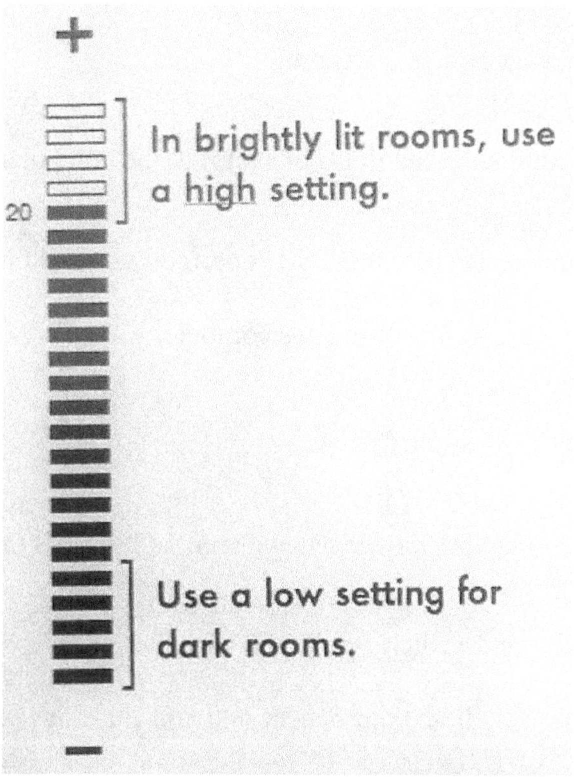

Problems With Wireless Connections

If you cannot download content using a wireless or 3G connection, make sure:

1. **Airplane Mode** is turned off on your device

2. Your battery charge is more than 40%

3. You are within range of the wireless network

Your Kindle Paperwhite Gets Stolen

If you misplace your device or your Kindle Paperwhite gets stolen, cancel your subscriptions through Manage Your Kindle. Your device cannot be unlocked easily if you've set up a passcode, but it is always better to file a police complaint.

Your Computer Does Not Recognize Kindle Paperwhite

1. Try connecting your device using a different USB port.

2. You can also restart your device and then connect it to the computer.

3. If you still face problems, make sure the USB is correctly inserted into your device and into the USB port on your Macintosh or Windows computer.

Your Battery Charge Drains Quickly

1. Make sure you are charging your device using a compatible USB cable.

2. Charge your tablet fully and switch off Wi-Fi when you don't want to use it. Remember, weak Wi-Fi connections can drain your battery and you'll always see low battery charge.

3. Sometimes USB ports on old computers do not have enough power to fully charge your device. If you have an old computer, you can buy a power adaptor to charge your device using a power outlet. The adaptor will fully charge your tablet in less than four hours.

4. Your battery life also depends on your screen brightness and the frequency of downloading content.

Resolving Content Issues

If you cannot receive content that is sent to your Send to Kindle email ID,

1. Make sure the sender's e-mail address is on your approved list.

2. Check that the Send-to-Kindle e-mail address you and your sender is using is correct.

3. Make sure that your Kindle Paperwhite is connected to Wi-Fi.

4. Check that your battery does not have a low charge

5. Confirm the attachment sent can be converted to supported formats including DOC, DOCX, RTF, JPEG, GIF, PNG, BMP, HTML, unprotected PDF and TXT.

Tips and Tricks

You No Longer Want to Receive Special Offers

If you want to unsubscribe from special offers on your Kindle Paperwhite, you'll have to make an extra payment to Amazon.

1. First connect your tablet to a Wi-Fi network.
2. Visit Manage your Kindle and then go to Manage your Devices.
3. Locate your Kindle Paperwhite and then click the tiny plus icon.
4. Click **Unsubscribe Special Offers.** This will put an end to special offers and Sponsored Screensavers that appear on your Kindle Paperwhite Home screen.
5. You'll then receive an e-mail notification that will confirm the further steps for unsubscribing from special offers.

Browsing the Web on Kindle Paperwhite

Many of you would be surprised to know that Kindle Paperwhite comes with an Experimental Web Browser that helps you to browse the internet. You can view most web pages on Paperwhite as the experimental browser supports JavaScript, SSL and cookies. However, you cannot access websites that use media plugins such as Flash, Java applets or Shockwave.

You can tap Menu from your Home Screen and then tap **Experimental Browser** to open the browser window. If you want to enter a specific web address or URL, tap the search box at the top of your screen.

Use the onscreen keyboard to enter your website address and then tap the arrow.

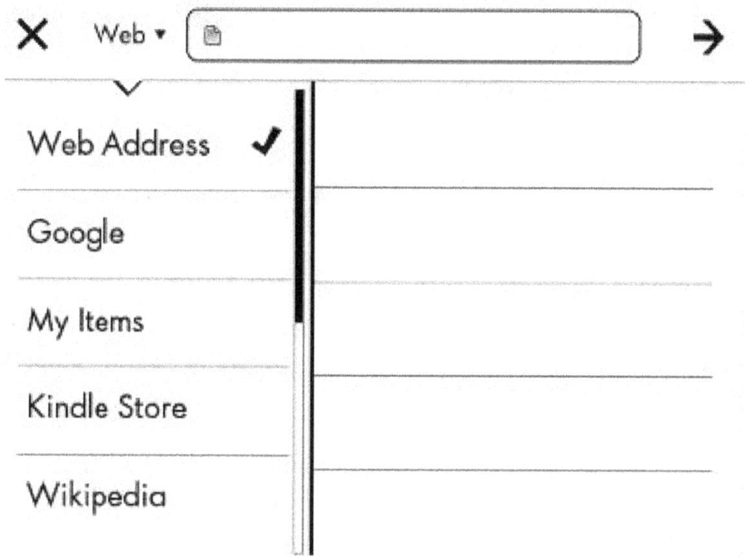

If you want to add a webpage to your bookmark list, first tap the Menu icon and then select **Bookmark this Page**. If you want to remove the bookmark later, tap the Menu icon and then tap **Bookmarks**. Select **Remove** and mark the box next to the bookmarks you want to remove. Tap **Remove** again to remove the bookmark from your list.

Tips for Maintaining Your Kindle Device

1. Do not use your Kindle Paperwhite in rain or wet locations.
2. Take care not to keep your device near food or liquid items. In case your device gets wet, unplug all cables and clean your Kindle Paperwhite using a soft dry cloth. Take care not to rub the screen with anything abrasive.
3. Use screen protectors and other covers to keep your device safe while traveling.
4. Don’t expose your tablet to extreme heat or cold.

5. Never attempt to clean your tablet with harsh chemicals or abrasive material.

6. Always use accessories that are compatible with your Kindle Paperwhite. It is good if you use the Amazon store to buy accessories for your device.

7. If you need to service your device, make sure you send it to Amazon Customer Support.

8. Always charge your tablet with the USB cable supplied with the device or a USB cable that is compatible with Kindle products.

9. Turn off your wireless connection when flying to prevent interference with aircraft system.

10. If your Kindle Paperwhite causes interference with other electronic devices, try to limit its use within the same region.

After reading this eBook, you should be fully aware of the interesting features offered by Kindle Paperwhite. You can now understand what exactly sets Paperwhite apart from other eBook readers that are available in the market. Don't forget to help your friends check out the most intriguing features of Kindle Paperwhite with the help of this eBook. Here's hoping that you've enjoyed reading this eBook and continue using your device with ease.